SUPER EFFECTIVE PLANNING

The Imperfect Guide for Effective Planning

That Works Quite Well Most of the Time

Nicco Krezdorn

TABLE OF CONTENTS

Life is what happens to you while you're busy making other plans.

– John Lennon

Intro

Time is wonderful. Time sucks.

The chances are high that you are flipping through this book (or even already bought it) because you are not happy with some organizational aspect of your current life. That makes us two already.

Ever since mankind invented the concept of time, we are running behind, desperately trying to stay in control over these countless moments, hours, days, months, and years that make up our life.

It's the old battle between what we want to have and achieve and what we can have and achieve at any given time.

If you are anything like me (would be cool if you were), then you have already tried a bunch of strategies to organize your life. Be it simple post-its, long lists, frustrating excel sheets, one-of-a-kind-but-still-sucking, or supposed-to-make-everything-easier-but-only-drive-you-crazy smartphone apps, calendar-sync-madness, and a bunch of other things.

I tried them all; they failed me all.

Another big problem I have with all the fantastic planning methods out there is this:

They typically address the modern-day knowledge worker or hipster entrepreneur. People that are to some extent in control of their time.

I haven't found anything that fits the need for someone employed in a high workload medical/academic setting.

If you work 12-14 hours a day, you typically don't have the time to color your daily planner according to your current emotions. If you have to use corporate software, email, calendars, and computers with restrictions and limitations that don't work cross-platform or sync with the latest app of the day, then you need something that brings it all together and just works.

After several years of trying and failing, I ended up with a mash-up of a number of techniques and self-made tools that now seem to work quite well for me and lots of people who ask me about it. It's not perfect – nothing is – but it works quite well, most of the time. Hence the subtitle of the book.

I'll be frank. I am not offering you the holy grail. Few things will be completely new, but the entire package hopefully will be. Some things will do wonders for you, while some won't. Take and use what you like and dump the rest.

I wrote this book to summarise what works for me – at least for now - so it may help at least one lost soul. I'll try to reduce salesy and annoying fluff talk as much as possible while keeping it as simple and somewhat entertaining as possible.

This book serves as a companion to the actual planning tool – the Super Effective Planner.

But you can use all the principles in it with a regular college block or note pad and a pen.

Please feel free to reach out with questions, suggestions, and feedback at any time.

Have fun with planning, failing, achieving approximately 50% of what you were aiming for (which is already pretty good), and starting all over again.

Cheers

Nicco

Who is this guy, and why should I listen to any word he says?

Good question.

I am currently working as an assistant professor for plastic and reconstructive surgery at Hannover Medical School, Germany, studying ex-vivo perfusion systems and plastic reconstructive allotransplantation. I have published 50+ scientific articles in renowned peer-reviewed papers (Pubmed).

I am the head of burn trauma surgery and clinically focus on reconstruction after trauma and nerve injury. I have written several book chapters on plastic and reconstructive surgeries and have given countless talks at national and international conferences.

In addition to my medical work, I write about effective strategies for healthy personal and work life.

I am running a small publishing house, working as a translator and author of several books, mostly in German.

Apart from that, I am working as a Yoga and Meditation teacher together with my wife at our joint online and offline yoga studio (yogarage.net).

I am performing as a semi-professional singer and saxophone player with my wedding band Swingshot (swingshot.de), as well as a DJ for electronic dance music.

I am a father of three fantastic kids and live and work in Germany.

Obviously, it takes some planning to keep all these things running, and since I have been asked quite frequently about how I actually do that – I thought I might as well write it down.

Keep what you like; toss the rest.

WHY PLAN

Who is in charge of your time?

Your family? Your friends? Your colleagues? Your boss? Your work?

In case you forgot, it's you.

And if you don't claim your time *or if you don't plan your time, someone else will.*

There's sort of a conundrum, a paradox, which is:

the more you plan, the more freedom you get.

And typically, people freak out when they hear this because they feel restrained or caged. But the most important thing within that context is: *you don't have to plan everything in detail.*

But what you do have to plan in order to get that freedom is the frame. You have to plan the frame, and the rest will take care of itself.

I have friends who refuse to plan their time because they want to stay "flexible" and "open to life." Very few of them – actually none – though enjoy the privilege of leading the lifestyle of a luxury bum with all the time, all the money, and no strings attached. The problem is, once one of these three elements goes missing, you are dependent and will have to plan.

The paradox of planned freedom.

Whatever the frame is for you – it will be different for everyone else.

In order to illustrate that concept, I want to share a quick story.

Back in 2013, I went on a break, and I decided to go to California, specifically to San Francisco, because I had this weird, wild idea in my head that if I get there, magic and especially crazy things will happen.

But I didn't plan anything.

I didn't even plan anything in terms of stay. I didn't call or text anyone. I didn't book a hotel. I didn't look out for anywhere to stay.

I thought it magically might just happen, and like in a road movie, I will meet random strangers who will let me sleep on their couch for free.

What happened, though, is that magically, nothing happened.

I ended up renting or booking overpriced same-day hotel rooms in rundown areas of San Francisco, where I was scared to walk at night. And then I tried to couch surf, which miserably failed because most hosts were only interested in single girls staying at their place.

I spent most of my days organizing the least costly way to sleep, which completely bummed me and made me super unhappy and semi-depressed. I could not at all appreciate anything of the California San Francisco vibe because I was busy taking care of my basic needs, which were food and shelter.

Once I realized that, I stopped. A friend of mine decided to come over on quick notice from Europe, and we decided to go on a road trip. But learning from my no-planning experiences, we decided to map out at least the rough points of where to go and where to stay by booking some Airbnb stays a couple of days ahead. Our frame. And it turned out to become exactly that weird, movie-like, crazy road trip because we were open enough to go with the flow and take all opportunities and experiences that presented themselves because we didn't have to take care of the basic stuff on a daily basis.

So that's what I mean by planning the frame. Make sure that the basic stuff is taken care of, that you know where you have to go and when you have to be there, what is required of you, whatever the context is, and whatever you're going for.

It gives you so much more freedom if these things are organized beforehand and taken care of. By doing this, you essentially take them off your mind, and that's the important part:

You don't have to carry all that around with you all day long.

Your planning clears your mind.

Everything that needs to be taken care of needs a place and a time.

And it doesn't matter if you want to take care of it or not.

Everything that needs to be taken care of needs a specific place and a specific time.

If you don't allocate that, you will be stressed, and there will be problems.

And once you both allocate a place and a time, all of that is gone, and you can go with the flow.

This is one of the essential pieces of effective planning.

Everything that needs to be taken care of needs a place and a time.

A Dream Without A Goal Is Just A Wish.

A Goal Without A Plan Is Just A Dream.

- unknown

WHAT TO PLAN

Life is chaos. Life always strives for order. Life yearns for control. Yet only a few achieve it temporarily.

It is one of our greatest delusions – the illusion of being in control.

Before we get too philosophical, let's try to keep it simple and boil it down to the essentials:

You should plan what you want to get.

You will fail partially, but that shouldn't keep you from trying.

Get rich or die tryin'

50 Cent

Why use the Super Effective Planner

I will spare you the detailed stories; let's just say I've tried them all.

Regular planners.

Motivational planners.

Spiritual planners

Lists.

Spreadsheets.

GTD.

Mindmaps.

Online tools. Hundreds of online tools.

Apps. Thousands of apps.

I read books on books, blogs, trainings, webinars, courses to find something that consistently works for me. Most failed acompletely, and some worked OK for a short time.

So, I kept what worked and put it all together in one system that has been working pretty well most of the time for a couple of years now.

It is essentially a system based on pen and paper. I am using a simple matrix that I kept drawing on college notebooks, day after day. But as I got tired of always having to draw my matrix manually, I decided to create a little book to save some time and graphite.

It checks a couple of boxes that are essential for me and my planning routine, as I will explain in more detail later.

- I can take it everywhere

- It fits in a pants' back pocket

- It fits basically in any pocket

- You don't have to charge it

- You don't need internet

- You don't need to sync

- You can easily change, erase, and add

- You can doodle

- You can draw, sketch, calculate and write

- Handwriting is pretty fast

- You can rip out pages

- It's like a swiss army knife – it's amazing what you can use a book and a pen for under different circumstances

- It's cheap

The chances are that not everything within this planning system and this planner will work perfectly for you. That's ok. As long as it works pretty well for you, you will get a lot of things done. And after all, that is what this is all about.

HOW TO PLAN

Big picture – goal setting

When you look at goals, the most important part of it is, once you have a goal, start with the end in mind. That is a concept that's been taken from the <u>Seven Habits of Highly Effective People</u>* by Stephen R. Covey, and I love that idea.

Imagine a goal to be a tombstone. When it (the project) is done, when it's finished, when it's buried, when it's over, look back and ask yourself:

How did you get there? How exactly do you get to that end?

And if you go backward and start with the end in mind and roll it up backward, that makes the steps much clearer than if you try to start from where you are at right now.

So, the important question is:

What is the end? Where do you want to go?

In life, at work, with your family, with yourself? Not necessarily in that order.

And what is your "Why?" Why do you want to go there?

This is important. If you don't have a "Why," it will be hard for you to get there. Because, why should you?

The parable of sailing

Goal setting is very similar to sailing. If you're on a sailing boat, chances are, you want to sail somewhere. Which means you have to plan where to go. So, the goal that you have, the end that you have in mind, is the harbor you want to arrive at.

To do that, you get yourself a map of the area where you are sailing. And you define that point where you want to go and mark it on the map. And then look at all the obstacles in the way, be it deep waters, sandbanks, islands, pirates, and whatnots. And then, you map out a route. Ideally backward. And there might be one or two or more different ways, how to get from the point where you are to the point where you want to get. And that's fine.

So, once you've looked at all the options, you decide which route you want to go. And that's your plan.

Now that you have a plan, you start sailing.

And then life happens.

Maybe the wind changes, there's an emergency, high tides, whatever it is, and you end up at some different island that wasn't on your plan altogether.

Or because of low winds, you couldn't get as far as you expected.

But that's not a bad thing. That's not the point. Because this is what life is all about. Aiming for something and trying to reach it, although in many cases, you won't reach it the first time - or you might never reach it. It's about the journey to that goal.

And then you end up at a completely different place, and this becomes your new starting point. It is for you to decide if the old goal is still the one you wanted to go for. Or maybe you figure out that the place where you are now is not that bad after all, and you don't have to go to that place that you initially thought you have to go to, and you adapt accordingly.

Many times, you will reach your initial goal though, rest assured.

If you have designed such a map, this map helps you

- to reorient yourself when you get lost

- to motivate you when you feel down

- to remind you that you are in charge and in power to decide what is important and what is not

- and to focus and plan ahead

5-3-1 years

We often overestimate how far we can get in the short term, or to stay with sailing, how far you get in one day.

But we do underestimate how far we can get in the long term, let's say, a sailing week.

Part of the problem is that we have a problem with grasping large numbers.

It's quite easy to imagine a year, 300 days. But it's hard to imagine what happens in three years, which is over 1,000 days.

Part of the reason for achieving more in the long run is that, over longer periods of time, if you consistently work on something, you get something like the compound effect on your work.

The more you work on it, the more the results compound, and this pays off the longer you do it. And that is why the results in the long-term future are much higher than you would expect them to be from where you are right now.

For that reason, I make 5-year plans, where I lay out my most ambitious outlandish goals. And then again, starting from that as the end in mind, I am breaking it down to a 3-year plan, a 1-year plan, and then further into 3-month plans.

Three months

A lot of studies have shown that the ideal planning horizon is 90 days or 3 months once you have mapped out your long-term plan.

The reason for three months is that it is a significantly long time to have a little bit of planning time ahead while simultaneously allowing for changes that happen in life and enable you to incorporate changes for the next quarter of your life.

All of that is then broken down into a) projects and b) areas. This is partially a concept of the PARA method of Tiago Forte. The key distinction that he rightly makes is that you have both projects and areas that require planning.

A project is something very specific, with a clear result and maybe date.

An area is an unspecific, broader, oftentimes ongoing process that should translate into specific projects/goals/tasks.

A project/goal is: get three 90 min. Thai massages this September

An area: Improve self-care.

Learning to distinguish the two is a key skill, to declutter your current to-do list of things that are too unspecific and therefore never get done.

Projects

A project is an endeavor to produce a specific result within a given time frame. It usually consists of multiple tasks and subtasks representing the specific steps to produce the end result.

Tasks

A task is the atomic micro-unit of planning. It should be a specific action, ideally with a clear objective, results, time frame, and date. You will have to break things down into smaller units until this point is reached.

The actual planning will take these atomic units and distribute them according to your priorities and time availabilities.

In summary, it comes down to this:

1. Define a goal

2. Start with the end in mind: Where do you want to go and why

3. Map backward from there in broad steps

4. Define the sub-steps and break them down to single item tasks

5. Distribute the tasks according to time and priority

Prioritizing

As mentioned earlier, we are not re-inventing the wheel here. Smarter people than me have come up with pretty good systems for prioritizing already. To name one that I like particularly is the so-called Eisenhower Matrix.

Essentially it is a matrix of the two-axis urgency and importance. You can place any given task in one of the four quadrants of this matrix. Most of your focus and planning should go to category 1 items: important and urgent items.

Second should come important but not-urgent items, as these will move the needle for you.

Third should be urgent but not-important items, and lastly, if at all not-urgent and not-important items.

Unfortunately, we typically tend to prioritize category 3 over category 2, which leads to great unhappiness.

While going through your plannable tasks, it is helpful to add a potential time estimate to allow for proper time allocation.

In order to move the needle towards the important but not urgent tasks that yield the most fruits for you – I can recommend classifying one of the category 2 tasks as the so-called "leapfrog" task. The "leapfrog" task is the task you avoid most (aka the frog you need to eat) that brings you forward (leap) the most. This task should be handled as if it would be category 1 – urgent and important.

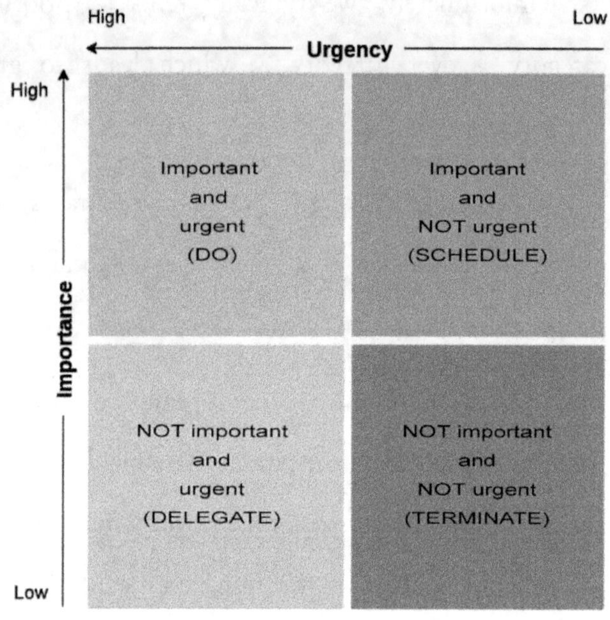
High
Low
Urgency
High
Importance
Important
and
urgent
(DO)
Important
and
NOT urgent
(SCHEDULE)
NOT important
and
urgent
(DELEGATE)
NOT important
and
NOT urgent
(TERMINATE)
Low

Habitualize it

I can't stretch the importance of habits and routines in your life, to lift the burden of the daily grind of things.

If you haven't read the **Power of Habit*** by Charles Duhigg, do it.

In a nutshell, a habit is a loop system of a cue followed by a routine leading to a reward. We all are creatures of habits. Though unconsciously established, most of them through prior experiences, family, friends, school, society, and marketing.

I use habits to prepare lunch and breakfast the night before, so I can use another habit for cooking fresh, healthy meals when I get up at 5 am in the morning. Other habits and routines help me to keep meditating and doing yoga on a daily basis early in the morning. I don't have to use mental energy to do these, because I would need to, and it wouldn't work because life is too complex and complicated and busy.

When you want to establish a new habit, do it deliberately and only tackle one at a time. Define it, prepare for it, and then keep it for 30 days. Because that is the time it takes for your mind and your homeostasis to adapt to it and make it an actual habit that lasts.

Delegate it

One of the more important lessons of evergreen wisdom I learned is this: I don't have to do everything myself. You don't have to be the CEO of a big company in order to be able to delegate tasks. Look around you. There might be co-workers who could take on the task, friends and family members, and the like. More often than not, delegation doesn't happen because of personal control issues than of appropriate delegatees. You might also want to hire someone for specific tasks.

A good exercise for this is to estimate or calculate your own hourly rate - you can also do that when you are employed – and then check if it is really the best use of your time and skill set to do the task yourself.

Going back to the Eisenhower Matrix, category 3 tasks – not-important but urgent tasks – are particularly well suited for delegation.

Focus it

You get most of your work done if you are able to work on something without interruption. Of course, that is not always possible. But it is your obligation to strive for uninterrupted chunks of time to focus. There is a whole concept behind it, called deep work (an excellent book on it here). The problem with all interruptions – however short – is that it takes you a certain amount of time to get back to where you were before the interruption. That is why the Super Effective Planner consists of chunks of 30 minutes. Whenever you work on something, turn off your phone, don't look at your smartphone, close any mail software, and in general, disable all notifications and widgets on your computer. Noise-canceling headphones are a wonderful additional tool to get into focus.

Principle of diminished friction

In order to start any task, you need to overcome the initial level of inertia. This is similar to the increased amount of energy necessary to move a standing car compared to keeping a running car moving.

This means you typically don't start certain tasks (especially the important but not urgent ones) because there is resistance towards that necessary amount of energy to start.

This holds particularly true for maintaining new habits.

One concept is to think about reducing or diminishing friction to lower the amount of energy needed.

As examples:

When writing a manuscript, always have the draft open on your computer with the cursor on the spot where you want to continue. Whenever you find time to work on it, you just open the laptop and continue writing instead of looking for the file and finding the area of focus.

Have your breakfast and or lunch prepared the day before, so you just have to heat it up to get a healthy meal.

Have all your files in a cloud that allows sharing/working when not at home.

Use apps, tools, widgets, among others, to prepare in such a way that you reduce friction wherever possible as much as possible.

Piggyback tasks to each other, for example, new habits to old habits – like brushing your teeth and meditation, so you always do when/after you do the other.

How to plan, using the Super Effective Planner

Super effective planning principles

-   Look at a 90-day time frame for areas of focus

-   Define one major goal per month per area

-   Plan in batches, blocks, and projects

-   Plan roughly on a weekly basis

-   Plan in detail on a daily basis

Goals

Our planner starts with an overview of your goals. And here you define your goals for this year, kind of the long-term goals, the island you want to go next to. Here, you define the goals for various areas of your life, be it work, personal development, family, finances.

And then you break these goals down to goals that can be achieved within three months. You do this for every specific area you chose. And then you define one goal per area per month that you want to achieve in one month in that area, and you write it down.

This helps you to keep an overview, a bird's eye view to always come back to and see what's important for you in that very month.

It helps you stay focused on a daily or weekly basis in a more granular fashion so that you align everything with where you want to go. It is your anchor to bring you back from the daily minutiae.

Goals

Year Goals

Goals for Month 1

Goals for Month 2

Goals for Month 3

The 3 months bird's eye view

This is a 15-week overview, where you can define

- significant events

- meetings

- birthdays

- things that are really important

- things that stand out that you want to have on your radar.

You can and should always go back to this overview when you do your weekly planning sessions, which we will touch later.

Week

Week

Week

Week

Week

Week

Week

Week

Week

Week

Week

Week

Week

Week

Week

Habits

The habit section is meant to house an overview of all of your current conscious habits that you define as important to you.

They are sectioned out for

- Daily habits (i.e., Morning Yoga)

- Weekly habits (i.e., Sunday Week Planning)

- Monthly habits (i.e., financial overview)

- Yearly habits (i.e., X-mas letter to yourself)

By filling these every time you start a new 3-month planner, you consciously revise your current habits, question them, refine them, toss the ones that don't work, and incorporate new ones.

Habits & Routines

Daily

Weekly

Monthly

Yearly

HABITS

	Monday	Tuesday	Wednesday	Thursday	Friday	Saturday	Sunday
5 am							
6 am							
7 am							
8 am							
9 am							
10 am							
11 am							
12 pm							
1 pm							
2 pm							
3 pm							
4 pm							
5 pm							
6 pm							
7 pm							
8 pm							
9 pm							
10 pm							
11 pm							

Now let's get to the nitty-gritty day to day planning.

Inbox

The inbox section is where you dump all tasks, ideas, projects, goals that come up over a day throughout the week.

The lines are separated to allow for early batching for different areas.

I tend to use the first inbox page for all medicine related things that come up. The second inbox page houses all other business, finance, family, personal, and other things.

You can and should use this section to already batch tasks and projects that have things in common. For example, mark calls that can be done on the commute. Or combine errands for different projects that can better be done at once.

Inbox

Week overview

This weekly overview is meant to serve as the birds-eye-view calendar for any given week. I block out sections for certain time frames (like hospital, kids, restaurant) without too much detail. This helps to see where your time is going.

As far as your control on your daily work tasks goes, try to again batch and combine things.

If you can schedule meetings or calls mostly on one day, so you can work with fewer interruptions on the other days. If you have writing to do, try to schedule it for one or two specific days; you get the point? The main goal is to get as much undivided and uninterrupted attention as possible for any given task.

This is the secret sauce to making you faster and more efficient.

If the first layer is identifying what to do, the second layer is defining when BEST to do it.

WEEK -

	Monday	Tuesday	Wednesday	Thursday	Friday	Saturday	Sunday
5 am							
6 am							
7 am							
8 am							
9 am							
10 am							
11 am							
12 pm							
1 pm							
2 pm							
3 pm							
4 pm							
5 pm							
6 pm							
7 pm							
8 pm							
9 pm							
10 pm							
11 pm							

Day-to-day

Every day has a 30-minute interval scaled timeline from 4 am in the morning to 11 pm in the evening.

The left side is to block out 30-minute chunks for specific tasks or batched tasks (more on that later). I also use it to visualize times of commuting/traveling/getting from point A to point B.

The right side is used to add details to certain tasks that don't fit in the left lines or that arise during meetings.

Underneath the phone icon, I note all unscheduled calls and text messages that I'd like to have over the day. The same goes for the mail icon for all emails, mails, and other messages.

The free space at the bottom serves for daily notes, doodles, observations, comments, and the like.

Not particularly rocket science, but it covers the essentials on one page.

Monday   / /

4.00 am	
4.30 am	
5.00 am	
5.30 am	
6.00 am	
6.30 am	
7.00 am	
7.30 am	
8.00 am	
8.30 am	
9.00 am	
9.30 am	
10.00 am	
10.30 am	
11.00 am	
11.30 am	
12.00 pm	
12.30 pm	
1.00 pm	
1.30 pm	
2.00 pm	
2.30 pm	
3.00 pm	
3.30 pm	
4.00 pm	
4.30 pm	
5.00 pm	
5.30 pm	
6.00 pm	
6.30 pm	
7.00 pm	
7.30 pm	
8.00 pm	
8.30 pm	
9.00 pm	
9.30 pm	
10.00 pm	
10.30 pm	
11.00 pm	

Throughout the day or at the end of the day

1. Every task that is accomplished is checked off in the inbox section.

2. Every unfinished task will be re-planned in the current week if necessary/possible or added to next week's inbox.

3. Every new task that arises will be planned in the current week if necessary/possible or added to next week's inbox.

The Notes Section

Not much to say here. A couple of clean white pages for notes. And there is always that moment when you need a piece of paper to rip out and hand to someone, so there you go.

These are the parts that make up the 3-month Super Effective Planner.

The heart of the actual Super Effective Planning process is the weekly planning ritual.

The Weekly Planning Ritual

This is the core part of effective planning.

It is a CRUCIAL part.

I do it typically on Sundays, and I recommend doing it before your new week starts.

The sequence that has proven most effective for me is as follows:

- Check 3-month overview

- Check last week's SEP inbox

- Check digital inbox (more on that later)

- Check physical inbox (more on that later)

- Check email inbox (un-tasked emails, more on that later)

- Check work calendar

- Check private/family calendar

    Then

- Break all of the above down to single tasks again

- Put all of these tasks on the new Inbox pages

- Batch them according to project and area

- Mark them (i.e., phone call, email, etc.)

- Prioritize them (according to Eisenhower Matrix, i.e., 1-4)

  Then

- Mark blocks of time-based on location in the weekly overview (work, home, meeting, etc.)

- Mark commute/travel time in between locations

  Then

- Transfer blocks to left sides of respective days in the day-to-day sections

- Add the tasks from inbox in 30-minute blocks for every day according to availability, time, and priority

- Use travel/commute blocks to plan for phone calls/messages.

- Transfer tasks that can't be scheduled realistically anymore to next week's inbox and move them up in the priority hierarchy (if applicable) or dump them entirely

That's it.

At first, it might look a little bit obsessive, repetitive, and exhausting. Once you get used to it, it typically can be done within 15-30 minutes.

The repetition is part of the concept as it makes you think about any given task multiple times and helps you clarify its importance and urgency.

Using a paper-based system allows for a couple of benefits for me:

- Speed, planning is much faster with pen and paper (trust me)

- You can easily erase, re-arrange, and add.

- Writing has been proven to enhance brain function and thinking, thus helping to think more clearly about your tasks.

It appears to be a clear process, but it will be messy.

And that is totally ok, as such is life.

No system, however intricate, intelligent, AI-based, sleekly-designed, will ever stay clean when actually used.

Things get dirty when you use them.

That is not a problem. The problem is cleaning them regularly so you can keep working with them.

Your planner will become messy. It will become dirty. Even physically, it should. It means you are using it properly.

That is why it is designed for a period of three months. Then you get a clean new one, so your tool always stays sharp and fresh.

APPENDIX

Tools

Obviously, I am not a caveman, fighting modern life with only a paper booklet and a pencil. In order to contain the daily corporate and personal madness, I am using various tools, apps, and services. (Some of the links are affiliate links, which means I might get paid a couple of cents when you sign up for a paid plan.)

Pencils

There is nothing like a sharp pencil, which is why I always have a family pack of sharp pencils like these PaperMateSharpWriters*.

Sketching (5-year) plans

I use <u>drafts.io</u> Google extension to map out my 5-year plans in a graphically pleasing way. It's free. I recently found <u>plectica.com</u> that I use similarly. As of now, I haven't made up my mind yet. I also use <u>Mindmeister</u>* for sketching mindmaps on certain topics.

Email

I recently moved to <u>Spark</u> because it handles all email providers such as Gmail, Microsoft Exchange, and my privately hosted ones. The main selling point for me is the ability to add emails as tasks to my digital inbox task program with a backlink to the original email. This allows me to wrestle my email inbox to zero while moving the mails that need some sort of reaction from me elsewhere.

Before that, I archived and deleted all emails so that only emails remained required a reaction. That worked pretty well but can get overwhelming fast if your habit of replying/reacting fails.

I further use <u>MailBackUpX</u> to have a searchable archive of all emails over time.

Digital Inbox/Planner

For a number of years, I used <u>Todoist</u>*, even achieving Enlightenment Status there. But the list view clogs up pretty fast, which is why I moved to <u>Meistertask.com</u>*, which has a fantastic Kanban interface, but requires slightly too many clicks to be really efficient. Nothing is perfect. Both integrate well with Spark, which was key. Both of them allow collaborative working and communication, which I use to run my publishing house as well as my research group.

Essentially, I use them to collect digital tasks, ideas, etc., from email, browsing, and for fast addition of ideas through my smartphone whenever the Super Effective Planner is not at hand.

During the Weekly Planning Ritual, I transfer/refer these tasks to the book planner's inbox section.

Calendars

I use Outlook Calendar for my work scheduling as it integrates with my mandatory outlook email client. I use Apple Calendar for a digital shared calendar with my wife.

And we use a 5-column monthly paper-based giant fridge-fixed calendar for the actual daily family planning. As long as they affect me, all of these events will be transferred manually to the Super Effective Planner during the Weekly Planning Ritual.

Archive/Resources/Data organization

Without going into too much detail and philosophical questions about Zettelkasten systems and the like – storing and accessing digital information is nowadays a crucial feature and question.

I use a wild mix of cross-platform cloud-based folder structures to save actual files.

I use **Dropbox*** for easy sharing and non-vital documents, iCloud for ease-of-use on my smartphone, **Google Drive*** for Business, **Owncloud** for my most personal content, stored on German and Swiss servers, corporate Owncloud for corporate files. They all share the same file system structure, which is inbox, projects, areas, archive, and resources.

For all things web-based, I used **Evernote*** for years as a dumb brain extension.

That goes along with **Instapaper** to read things later that don't necessarily have to be stored (emails, articles, blog posts, etc.).

10x Lifestyle Habit Changes

There are a few things lifestyle-wise that changed my life significantly for the better. As this is not a lifestyle guide, I will only briefly touch upon them. If you are interested in more details of any of these, feel free to reach out and let me know.

Yoga

I am both practicing and teaching a mix of Vinyasa-Yoga and Kundalini-Yoga as the mix of both worlds – stripped from any spiritual overhead – works magic for my physical, mental, emotional, and yes also spiritual wellbeing. I created a modular 5-45-minute best-of Yoga flow that I call Super Effective Yoga (surprise), that I practice daily for about 15 minutes.

Super Easy Start: Google Yoga Down-Dog Pose, practice that for 5 minutes daily, and you are off to a perfect start.

Or join us at yogarage.net

Meditation

I moved from various techniques through Vipassana-Meditation to Kryia-Meditation, all of which I highly recommend. Surprisingly I came up with my own little mash-up technique that incorporates what worked best for me from all techniques.

Super Easy Start: Take it from Buddha himself:

- Sit Down

- Close Your Eyes

- Watch Your Breath

Nutrition

Don't eat shit. Everyone knows what shit is. If you can't pronounce the ingredients, don't eat it. If it sounds like chemicals, don't eat it. Don't eat anything that requires a lot of production techniques. I am all for a vegetarian Mediterranean diet without becoming apologetic and dogmatic about it.

Drink more water. Warm water.

If coffee then espresso, if tea then green tea.

Sleep

Sleep in a completely dark room, no technical devices in your bedroom, and open your window. Use your bed for sleeping and co-sleeping only.

Relationships

Read <u>Radical Honesty</u>* by Brad Blanton. Practice Radical Honesty. That's pretty much all you need.

FAMOUS LAST WORDS

Don't take any of my words for anything. Try everything for yourself. Keep what works, keep what you like, toss the rest.

Life is messy, embrace it, accept it, and keep failing forward while trying to control it for a while.

Have fun with your life and with whatever you do.

I would love to hear about your experiences, and I would love to get your feedback. Please feel free to reach out to me anytime.

Best

Nicco